Pies & Tarts

A Delicious Slice of Life

COOKBOOK

Dessert Dreamweaver

Table of Contents

Pies & Tarts
A Delicious Slice of Life
DessertDreamweaver

Copyright

P ies & Tarts A Delicious Slice of Life
First edition. March, 2024.
Copyright © 2024 Dessert Dreamweaver.
Written by Dessert Dreamweaver.
DessertDreamweaver@gmail.com
All rights reserved. No part of this book may be reproduced, stored in a retrieval system, or transmitted in any form or by any means—electronic, mechanical, photocopying,

recording, or otherwise—without the prior

written permission of the publisher.

Dessert Dreamweaver

About the Author

The publisher boasts over twenty years of experience within the confectionery sector,
having operated within esteemed international hotel chains, several
confectionery factories, and diverse retail
outlets. Their extensive expertise in this
captivating industry is widely admired and
cherished by many.
DessertDreamweaver@gmail.com

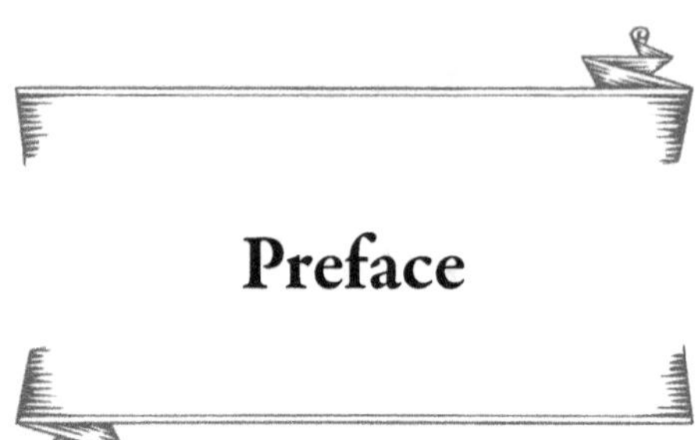

Preface

Welcome to a culinary journey that celebrates one of the most beloved and versatile delights in the world of baking: tarts and pies. From the flaky crusts to the luscious fillings, these delectable treats have been enchanting taste buds for centuries, transcending cultures and cuisines to become cherished staples on dining tables around the globe.

In this cookbook, we invite you to explore the artistry and creativity of tart and pie making. Whether you're an experienced baker looking to expand your repertoire or a novice eager to dive into the world of pastry, there's something here for everyone. From classic recipes passed down through generations to innovative twists that push the boundaries of tradition, each dish is crafted with care and precision to deliver a symphony of flavors in every bite.

But tarts and pies are more than just desserts; they're a canvas for culinary expression. Here, you'll discover a diverse array of sweet and savory creations that

showcase the versatility of this humble pastry. From rustic fruit-filled galettes to elegant custard tarts adorned with seasonal produce, each recipe offers a glimpse into the endless possibilities of tart and pie making.

. It is our sincere desire that this publication proves fulfilling to you .

.

Tarte aux Pommes

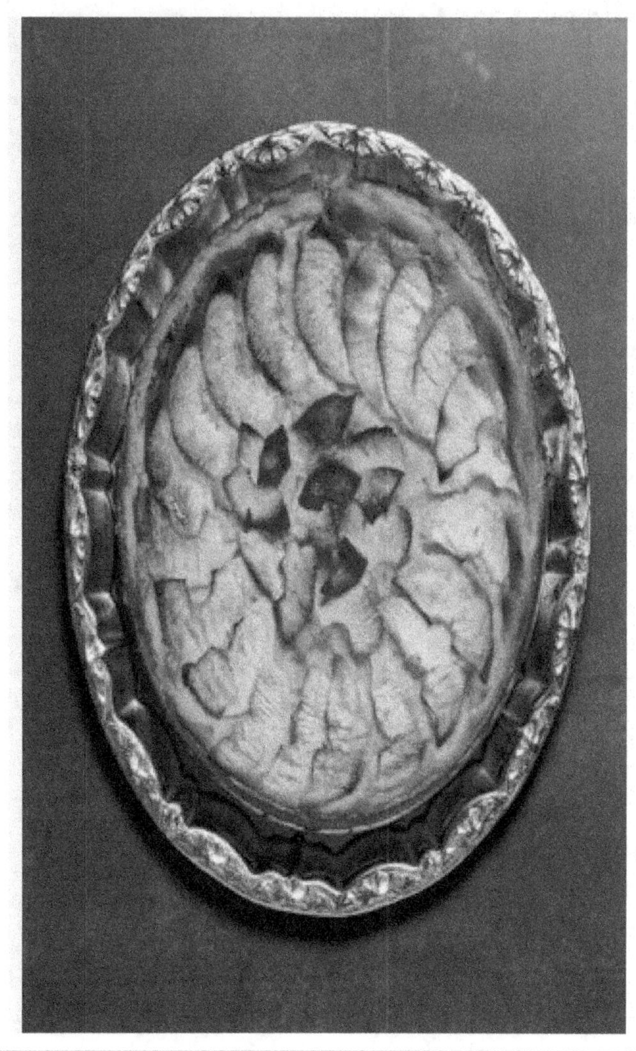

The most famous type of tart au pie is likely the "Tarte aux Pommes," which is French for apple tart. It's a classic French dessert made with thinly sliced apples arranged in a pastry crust and often glazed with apricot jam or caramel for a shiny finish. Tarte aux Pommes is beloved for its simplicity, elegance, and delicious flavor profile, making it a favorite in French patisseries and households alike

. Ingredients:

For the pastry:

300g all-purpose flour

1/4 teaspoon salt

150g unsalted butter, cold and diced

100g granulated sugar

1 large egg

1 teaspoon vanilla extract

2 tablespoons cold water

For the filling:

4 medium-sized apples

2 tablespoons lemon juice

100g granulated sugar

1/2 teaspoon ground cinnamon (optional)

Apricot jam or honey, for glazing (optional)

2 large eggs

1 teaspoon vanilla extract

50g unsalted butter melted

Instructions:

Prepare the pastry:

In a large mixing bowl, combine the flour, salt,
and sugar. Add the cold, diced butter.

Using your fingertips or a pastry cutter, rub the
butter into the flour mixture until it resembles coarse breadcrumbs.

In a small bowl, whisk together the eggs vanilla and cold water.
Pour this mixture into the flour-butter mixture.

Mix until the dough comes together. If it's too dry, add a little more
water, one teaspoon at a time.

Shape the dough into a ball, flatten it slightly into a disk, wrap it in
plastic wrap, and refrigerate for at least 30 minutes.

Prepare the filling:

Peel, core, and thinly slice the apples. Toss them in a bowl with lemon juice to prevent browning.

In a separate bowl, mix together the sugar

egge.butter and cinnamon. (if using).

Assemble the tart:

Preheat your oven to 375°F (190°C).

On a lightly floured surface, roll out the chilled pastry dough into a circle, about 1/8 inch thick.

Transfer the rolled-out dough to a tart pan or pie dish, pressing it gently into the bottom and up the sides. Trim any excess dough.

Arrange the sliced apples in overlapping concentric circles on top of the pastry. Sprinkle the cinnamon-sugar.eggs mixture evenly over the apples.

Bake the tart:

Place the tart in the preheated oven and bake for 30-40 minutes, or until the pastry is golden brown and the apples are tender.

If desired, warm apricot jam or honey in a small saucepan and brush it over the top of the tart for a shiny glaze.

Allow the tart to cool slightly before serving.

Serve:

Serve the Tarte aux Pommes warm or at room temperature. Optionally, you can accompany it with a scoop of vanilla ice cream or a dollop of whipped cream.

Enjoy your delicious homemade Tarte aux Pommes!

Cheesecake pie

Originating in ancient Greece, the cheesecake has traveled centuries, evolving into the delightful dessert we know today

.

Ingredients:
For the crust:
150g graham cracker crumbs
90g. unsalted butter, melted
50g.granulated sugar
For the filling:
450g cream cheese, softened
120g granulated sugar
1 large eggs
1 teaspoon vanilla extract
50g sour cream
50g.blueberries (optional)
Instructions:
1. Preheat the oven to 350°F (175°C).

2. In a mixing bowl, combine the graham cracker crumbs, melted butter, and 50g of sugar. Mix until the crumbs are evenly coated with butter.

3. Press the crumb mixture into the bottom and up the sides of a 9-inch pie dish to form the crust. Use the back of a spoon or a flat-bottomed measuring cup to press the crumbs firmly.

4. In a separate mixing bowl, beat the cream cheese and 120g of sugar together until smooth and creamy.

5. Add the eggs one at a time, mixing well after each addition.

6. Stir in the vanilla extract and sour cream until well combined.

7. Pour the filling into the prepared crust, spreading it evenly with a spatula.

8. Bake the cheesecake pie in the preheated oven for 30-35 minutes, or until the filling is set and the edges are lightly golden.

9. Remove the pie from the oven and let it cool completely on a wire rack.

10. Once cooled, refrigerate the cheesecake pie for at least 4 hours, or overnight, to allow it to set fully.

11. Serve slices of cheesecake pie plain or with your favorite topping, such as fresh fruit, fruit compote, whipped cream, or chocolate sauce.

Enjoy your delicious homemade cheesecake pie!

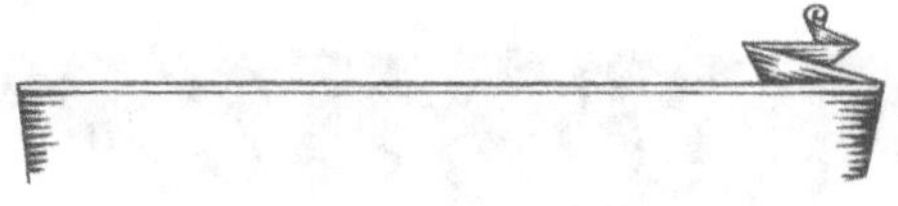

Caramel Pear Tart

P ears, with their luscious sweetness and delicate texture, have been cherished in French cuisine for centuries. In the late 19th and early 20th centuries, as sugar became more accessible and caramelization techniques advanced, chefs began to experiment with combining pears and caramel in various desserts.

The caramel pear tart emerged as a masterpiece of this experimentation – a harmonious marriage of caramelized sugar and tender, ripe pears nestled atop a flaky, buttery crust. Its popularity spread rapidly, enchanting diners with its simplicity and sophistication.

Ingredients:

For the pastry crust:

300g all-purpose flour

150g unsalted butter, cold and diced

100g granulated sugar

2 egg yolk

2 tablespoons cold water

For the filling:

4 ripe pears, peeled, cored, and thinly sliced

100g granulated sugar

70g unsalted butter

50g cup heavy cream

1 teaspoon vanilla extract

Pinch of salt

Instructions:

1. Prepare the Pastry Crust:

In a food processor, pulse together the flour, butter, and sugar until the mixture resembles coarse crumbs.

Add the egg yolk and cold water, then pulse until the dough comes together. Be careful not to overmix.

Shape the dough into a disk, wrap it in plastic wrap, and refrigerate for at least 30 minutes.

2. Preheat the Oven:

Preheat your oven to 375°F (190°C).

3. Roll out the Pastry:

On a floured surface, roll out the chilled pastry dough into a circle large enough to fit into your tart pan.

Carefully transfer the rolled-out dough to the tart pan, pressing it gently into the bottom and up the sides. Trim any excess dough.

4. Prepare the Filling:

In a saucepan, melt the butter over medium heat. Add the sugar and cook, stirring constantly, until the sugar has melted and turned a golden caramel color.

Slowly pour in the heavy cream while stirring continuously. Be careful as the mixture will bubble up.

Remove the caramel from heat and stir in the vanilla extract and salt.

Arrange the sliced pears evenly over the pastry crust.

Pour the caramel sauce over the pears, ensuring they are well coated.

5. Bake the Tart:

Place the tart in the preheated oven and bake for 35-40 minutes, or until the crust is golden brown and the caramel is bubbly.

6. Serve:

Allow the tart to cool slightly before serving. You can serve it warm or at room temperature. Optionally, you can serve with a scoop of vanilla ice cream or a dollop of whipped cream for an extra indulgent treat.

Enjoy your delicious Caramel Pear Tart!

oreo pie

Oreo pie is a delicious dessert made primarily from Oreo cookies and cream. There are many variations of Oreo pie recipes, but a common one involves crushing Oreo cookies to form a crust, mixing the crushed cookies with butter, and then pressing the mixture into a pie dish to form the base. The filling typically consists of a mixture of cream cheese, sugar, vanilla extract, and whipped cream or Cool Whip, often folded together with crushed Oreo cookies. Some recipes also incorporate additional ingredients like chocolate ganache or chocolate chips for added flavor.

Oreo pie is a delicious dessert made with a crust of crushed Oreo cookies and a creamy filling usually made from whipped cream, cream cheese, and crushed Oreos. It's a popular dessert choice for those who love the classic combination of chocolate and cream. Here's a simple recipe to make Oreo pie:

Ingredients:

For the crust:

24 Oreo cookies

5 tablespoons unsalted butter, melted

For the filling:

250g cream cheese, softened

100g granulated sugar

1 teaspoon vanilla extract

450ml heavy cream

12 Oreo cookies, crushed

Instructions:

Prepare the crust:

Preheat your oven to 350°F (175°C).

In a food processor, crush the Oreo cookies into fine crumbs.

In a mixing bowl, combine the Oreo crumbs with melted butter until well mixed.

Press the mixture evenly into the bottom and up the sides of a 9-inch pie dish.

Bake the crust for 8-10 minutes, then let it cool completely.

Make the filling:

In a large mixing bowl, beat the softened cream cheese until smooth.

Add sugar and vanilla extract, and beat until well combined and creamy.

In a separate bowl, whip the heavy cream until stiff peaks form.

Gently fold the whipped cream into the cream cheese mixture until well combined.

Fold in the crushed Oreo cookies.

Assemble the pie:

Pour the filling into the cooled Oreo crust, spreading it out evenly.

Smooth the top with a spatula.

Optional: Garnish the top with additional crushed Oreo cookies if desired.

Chill the pie:

Refrigerate the Oreo pie for at least 4 hours, or until set.

Serve:

Once the pie is chilled and set, slice and serve cold.

You can optionally top each slice with whipped cream or a drizzle of chocolate syrup for extra indulgence.

Enjoy your delicious homemade Oreo pie!

shoofly pie

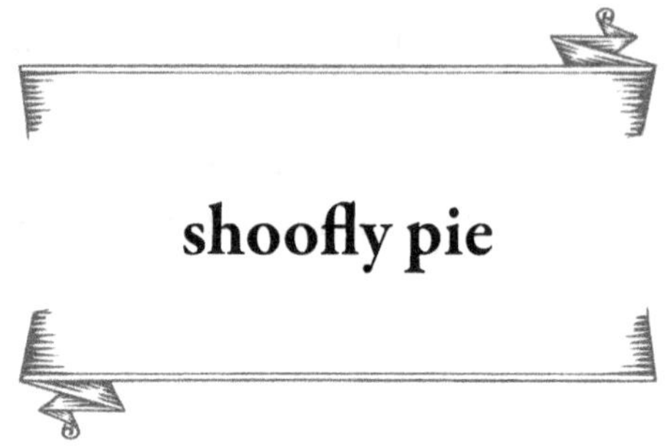

S hoofly pie is a traditional American dessert that originated among the Pennsylvania Dutch in the 1800s. It is a type of molasses pie

with a crumbly topping, and it's often associated with the Pennsylvania Dutch culture.

The pie typically consists of a pie crust filled with a mixture of molasses, brown sugar, and sometimes a bit of flour and water. The crumbly topping is made from a mixture of flour, brown sugar, and butter. When baked, the molasses filling becomes gooey and rich, while the topping adds a crunchy texture.

Shoofly pie is often served as a dessert, either warm or cold, and it pairs well with a dollop of whipped cream or a scoop of vanilla ice cream. It's a nostalgic and comforting dessert, particularly popular in regions with strong Pennsylvania Dutch influences.

Ingredients:

For the Pie Crust:

350g all-purpose flour

½ teaspoon salt

150g unsalted butter, chilled and cubed

50g granulated sugar

2-4 tablespoons ice water

For the filling:

1 cup dark molasses

3/4 cup boiling water

1 teaspoon baking soda

1 egg, beaten

For the crumb topping:

300g all-purpose flour

200g packed light brown sugar

70g unsalted butter, cold and cut into small pieces

1/2 teaspoon ground cinnamon

1/4 teaspoon ground ginger

Instructions:

1. Prepare the Pie Crust:

In a large mixing bowl, combine the.sugar flour and salt.

Add the chilled, cubed butter and mix until the mixture resembles coarse crumbs.

Gradually add the ice water, one tablespoon at a time, mixing until the dough comes together.

Shape the dough into a disk, wrap it in plastic wrap, and refrigerate for at least 30 minutes.

2. Preheat the oven:

Preheat your oven to 375°F (190°C).

3. Roll out the crust:

On a floured surface, roll out the chilled dough into a circle large enough to fit into a 9-inch pie dish.

Carefully transfer the dough to the pie dish, pressing it gently into the bottom and sides. Trim any excess dough from the edges.

4. Prepare the Filling:

In a small bowl, mix together the molasses and boiling water until well combined. Stir in the baking soda until dissolved. Let the mixture cool slightly.

Once the molasses mixture has cooled slightly, stir in the beaten egg until fully incorporated.

In another bowl, prepare the crumb topping by mixing together the flour. Cinnamon. ginger .and brown sugar. Cut in the cold butter using a pastry cutter or fork until the mixture resembles coarse crumbs. Set aside.

Pour the molasses filling into the prepared pie crust.

Sprinkle the crumb topping evenly over the molasses filling.

Place the pie on a baking sheet to catch any drips, and bake in the preheated oven for 10 minutes.

After 10 minutes, reduce the oven temperature to 350°F (175°C) and continue baking for an additional 35-40 minutes, or until the filling is set and the crust is golden brown.

Remove the pie from the oven and allow it to cool completely on a wire rack before serving.

Serve slices of shoofly pie on their own or with a dollop of whipped cream or a scoop of vanilla ice cream, if desired.

Additional Step for Layered Topping:

Before pouring the molasses filling into the pie crust, spread about half of the crumb topping mixture evenly over the bottom of the crust. Then, pour the molasses filling over the crumb layer. Finally, sprinkle the remaining crumb topping over the molasses filling as instructed in the original recipe.

This additional step adds an extra dimension of flavor and texture to the pie, making it even more indulgent. Adjust the amount of crumb topping you use for the bottom layer according to your preference, keeping in mind that it should provide a solid base for the molasses filling to sit on.

Enjoy your homemade shoofly pie!

blueberry pie

In this recipe, we embark on a journey to recreate that classic blueberry pie experience. From selecting the freshest berries to crafting the perfect pastry, each step is imbued with care and attention to detail. Whether you're a seasoned baker or a novice in the kitchen, this recipe promises to guide you through the process, ensuring a delicious outcome that will leave your taste buds singing.

Ingredients:

For the crust:

500g all-purpose flour

1 teaspoon salt

5 teaspoon granulated sugar

150g unsalted butter, cold and cut into small cubes

1 large egg, beaten

1/4 to 1/2 cup ice water

For the filling:

5 cups fresh blueberries, washed and drained

200g granulated sugar

75g cornstarch

1 tablespoon lemon juice

1 teaspoon lemon zest

1/2 teaspoon ground cinnamon

1/4 teaspoon salt

1 tablespoon unsalted butter, cut into small pieces

Instructions:

Preheat your oven to 375°F (190°C).

To make the crust, in a large mixing bowl, combine the flour, salt, and sugar. Add the cold butter cubes and use a pastry cutter or your fingers to cut the butter into the flour mixture until it resembles coarse crumbs.

Slowly add the egg and ice water, 1 tablespoon at a time, mixing with a fork, until the dough starts to come together. Be careful not to add too much water. Once the dough begins to hold together, gather it into a ball, divide it in half, and flatten each half into a disk. Wrap each disk in plastic wrap and refrigerate for at least 30 minutes.

While the dough chills, prepare the filling. In a large bowl, combine the blueberries, sugar, cornstarch, lemon juice, lemon zest, cinnamon, and salt. Toss until the blueberries are well coated.

Roll out one disk of dough on a lightly floured surface into a circle large enough to fit into a 9-inch pie dish. Transfer the dough to the pie dish and gently press it into the bottom and sides.

Pour the blueberry filling into the crust, spreading it out evenly. Dot the filling with pieces of butter.

Roll out the second disk of dough and place it over the filling. Trim any excess dough and crimp the edges to seal. Cut a few slits in the top crust to allow steam to escape.

Place the pie on a baking sheet to catch any drips and bake in the preheated oven for 50 to 60 minutes, or until the crust is golden brown and the filling is bubbly.

Allow the pie to cool completely before serving. Serve slices with a scoop of vanilla ice cream, if desired. Enjoy your homemade blueberry pie!

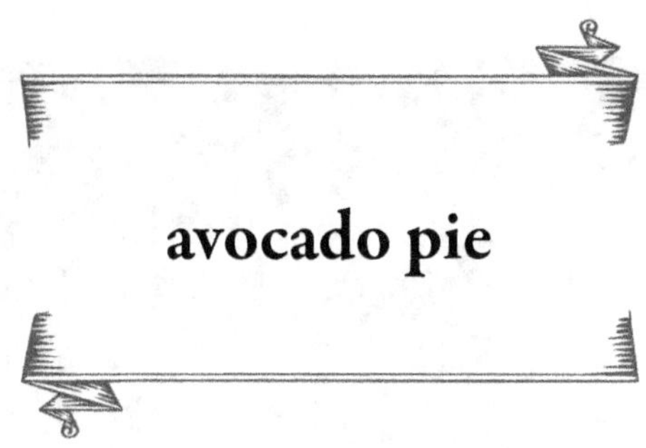

avocado pie

Avocado pie is a unique dessert that might sound unusual but is surprisingly delicious. It's made with avocados, which lend their creamy texture and subtle flavor to the pie. Here's a basic recipe to make avocado pie:

Ingredients:

2 ripe avocados

1/2 cup sweetened condensed milk

1/4 cup fresh lime or lemon juice

1 teaspoon vanilla extract

1 pre-made graham cracker pie crust

Whipped cream (optional, for serving)

green color) Optional(

Instructions:

Scoop out the flesh of the avocados and place them in a blender or food processor.

Add the sweetened condensed milk, lime or lemon juice, and vanilla extract to the blender.

Blend the mixture until smooth and creamy. You may need to stop and scrape down the sides of the blender or food processor to ensure all ingredients are well combined.

Once the mixture is smooth, pour it into the pre-made graham cracker pie crust.

Smooth out the top of the pie filling with a spatula or the back of a spoon.

Refrigerate the pie for at least 2 hours, or until set.

Once chilled and set, remove the pie from the refrigerator and slice it into servings.

Serve the avocado pie chilled, topped with whipped cream if desired.

This avocado pie is a refreshing and unique dessert that's perfect for avocado lovers or anyone looking to try something new!

fruit tart

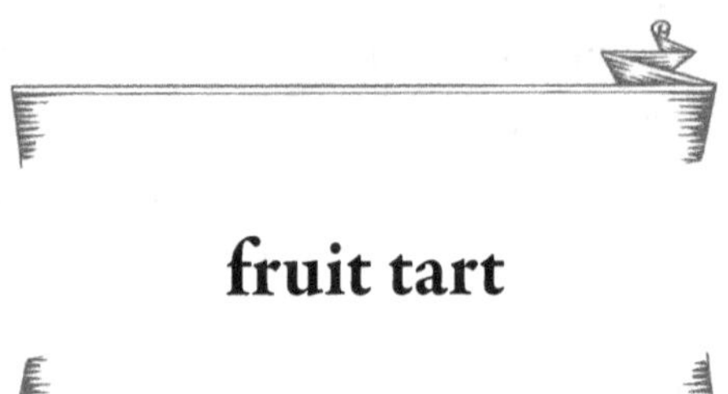

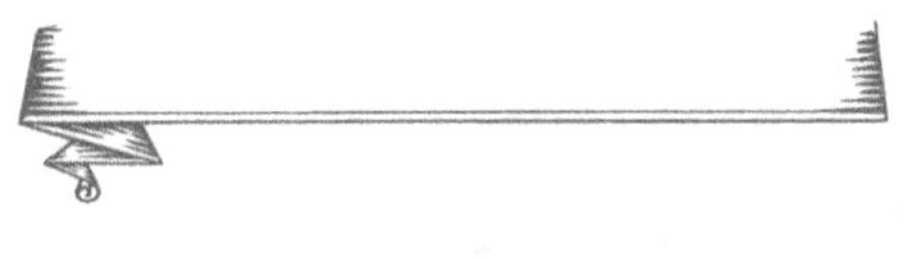

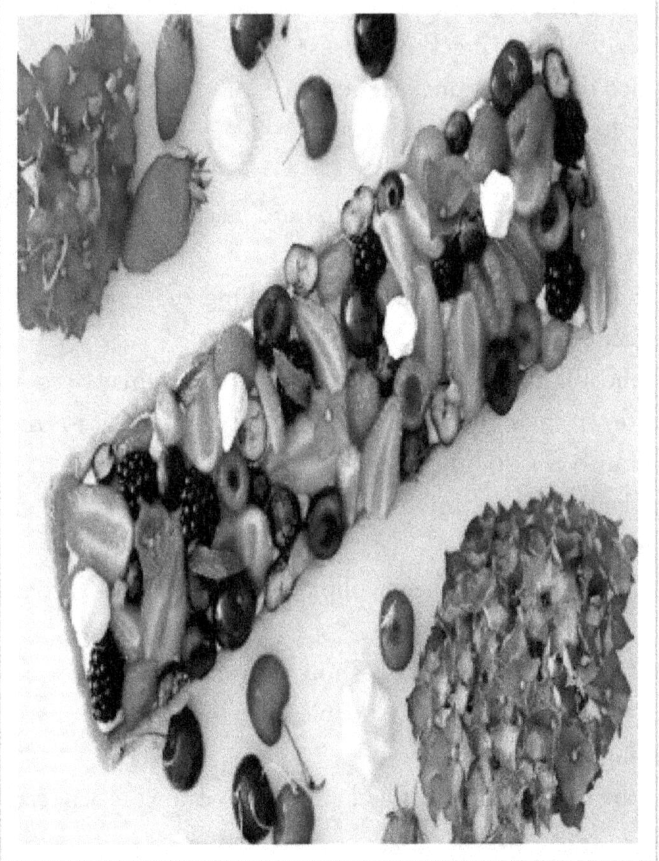

A fruit tart is a delightful dessert consisting of a pastry crust filled with pastry cream or custard and topped with fresh fruits, such as strawberries, kiwi, blueberries, raspberries, or any other seasonal fruit.

The crust can be made from shortcrust pastry or puff pastry, and the pastry cream is often flavored with vanilla. Fruit tarts are popular in many cuisines around the world and are often served chilled. They are not only visually appealing but also offer a perfect balance of sweetness and freshness from the fruits.

Ingredients:

For the pastry crust:

300g all-purpose flour

200g unsalted butter, cold and cut into small pieces

100g granulated sugar

1 egg yolk

1-2 tablespoons cold water

For the pastry cream:

1 1/2 cups whole milk

1/3 cup granulated sugar

3 egg yolks

2 tablespoons cornstarch

1 teaspoon vanilla extract

For the fruit topping:

Assorted fresh fruits (such as strawberries, kiwi, blueberries, raspberries, etc.)

Apricot jam or jelly for glazing

Instructions:

Prepare the pastry crust:

In a mixing bowl, combine the flour and sugar.

Add the cold butter pieces and rub them into the flour mixture using your fingertips until it resembles coarse breadcrumbs.

Add the egg yolk and 1 tablespoon of cold water. Mix until the dough comes together, adding more water if needed.

Shape the dough into a disk, wrap it in plastic wrap, and refrigerate for at least 30 minutes.

Preheat your oven:

Preheat your oven to 375°F (190°C).

Roll out the pastry dough:

On a lightly floured surface, roll out the chilled pastry dough into a circle large enough to fit your tart pan.

Carefully transfer the rolled-out dough to a tart pan, pressing it gently into the bottom and sides.

Trim any excess dough hanging over the edges.

Blind bake the pastry crust:

Line the pastry crust with parchment paper or aluminum foil, and fill it with pie weights, dried beans, or rice to prevent it from puffing up during baking.

Bake in the preheated oven for about 15-20 minutes, or until the crust is lightly golden.

Remove the weights and parchment paper, and let the crust cool completely.

Prepare the pastry cream:

In a saucepan, heat the milk over medium heat until it reaches a simmer.

In a separate bowl, whisk together the sugar, egg yolks, and cornstarch until smooth.

Gradually pour the hot milk into the egg mixture while whisking continuously.

Return the mixture to the saucepan and cook over medium heat, stirring constantly, until it thickens.

Remove from heat and stir in the vanilla extract. Let the pastry cream cool slightly.

Assemble the tart:

Spread the pastry cream evenly over the cooled pastry crust.

Arrange the fruit topping:

Wash and prepare your choice of fresh fruits. Slice larger fruits like strawberries and kiwi.

Arrange the fruits on top of the pastry cream in an attractive pattern.

Glaze the tart:

Heat the apricot jam or jelly in a small saucepan until melted.

Brush the melted jam over the arranged fruits to give them a glossy finish.

Chill and serve:

Refrigerate the fruit tart for at least 1 hour before serving to allow the pastry cream to set.

Slice and serve the tart chilled. Enjoy!

Feel free to customize the fruit selection or experiment with different flavors for the pastry cream to suit your taste preferences.

pumpkin pie

Pumpkin pie is a traditional dessert often associated with fall and Thanksgiving in North America. It's made primarily with pumpkin puree, sweetened condensed milk, eggs, and a blend of spices like cinnamon, nutmeg, and cloves, all poured into a pie crust and baked until set. The pie is typically served chilled or at room temperature, sometimes topped with whipped cream. It's a beloved dessert for many due to its warm, spiced flavor and creamy texture.

Ingredients for the Pie Crust:

250g all-purpose flour

1/2 teaspoon salt

100g (1 stick) unsalted butter, chilled and cut into small cubes

3 to 4 tablespoons ice water

Ingredients for the Pumpkin Filling:

1 (15-ounce) can pumpkin puree

1 (14-ounce) can sweetened condensed milk

2 large eggs

1 teaspoon ground cinnamon

1/2 teaspoon ground ginger

1/2 teaspoon ground nutmeg

1/2 teaspoon salt

Instructions for the Pie Crust:

In a large mixing bowl, combine the all-purpose flour and salt.

Add the chilled, cubed butter to the flour mixture. Using a pastry blender or your fingertips, work the butter into the flour until the mixture resembles coarse crumbs with pea-sized pieces of butter.

Gradually add the ice water, 1 tablespoon at a time, tossing the mixture with a fork after each addition. Continue adding water until the dough starts to come together.

Gather the dough into a ball, then flatten it into a disk. Wrap the dough in plastic wrap and refrigerate for at least 30 minutes (or up to 2 days).

After chilling, remove the dough from the refrigerator and let it sit at room temperature for a few minutes to soften slightly.

On a lightly floured surface, roll out the dough into a circle about 12 inches in diameter. Carefully transfer the rolled-out dough to a 9-inch pie dish. Press the dough gently into the bottom and sides of the dish, trimming any excess dough from the edges.

Instructions for the Pumpkin Filling:

Preheat your oven to 425°F (220°C).

In a large mixing bowl, whisk together the pumpkin puree, sweetened condensed milk, eggs, spices (cinnamon, ginger, nutmeg), and salt until well combined.

Pour the pumpkin mixture into the unbaked pie crust, spreading it out evenly.

Place the pie in the preheated oven and bake for 15 minutes.

After 15 minutes, reduce the oven temperature to 350°F (175°C) and continue baking for an additional 35 to 40 minutes, or until the pie is set and a knife inserted near the center comes out clean.

Once done, remove the pie from the oven and allow it to cool completely on a wire rack.

Once cooled, refrigerate the pie for at least 2 hours or until chilled.

Serve the pumpkin pie slices cold or at room temperature, optionally topped with whipped cream.

Enjoy your homemade pumpkin pie with a delicious, flaky crust!

pecan pie

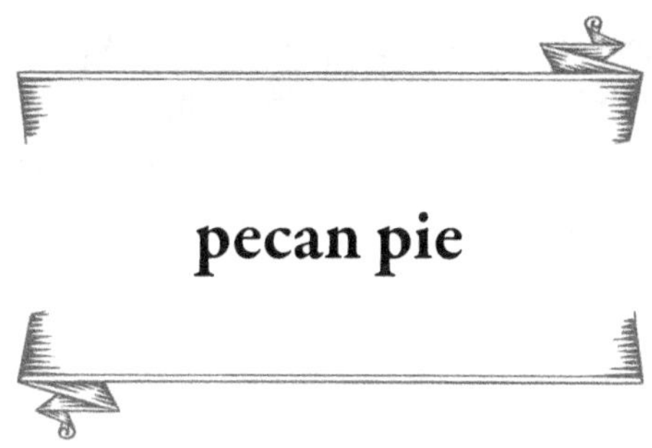

Pecan pie is a classic American dessert that consists of a sweet filling made primarily of pecans, sugar, corn syrup, eggs, and butter, all baked in a pie crust. It's particularly popular during the fall and winter months, often served at holiday gatherings like Thanksgiving and Christmas. Pecan pie is known for its rich, gooey filling and nutty flavor, which comes from the pecans. It's typically served warm or at room temperature, sometimes with a dollop of whipped cream or a scoop of vanilla ice cream on top.

Ingredients:

For the crust:

250g all-purpose flour

1/2 teaspoon salt

125g unsalted butter, cold and cut into small cubes

2-4 tablespoons ice water

For the filling:

200g light corn syrup

200g packed brown sugar

3 large eggs

70g unsalted butter, melted

1 teaspoon vanilla extract

1/4 teaspoon salt

250g pecan halves

Instructions:

Prepare the crust: In a large mixing bowl, combine the flour and salt. Add the cold butter cubes and use a pastry cutter or your fingertips to work the butter into the flour until the mixture resembles coarse crumbs.

Gradually add the ice water, 1 tablespoon at a time, mixing with a fork until the dough just begins to come together. Be careful not to overwork the dough.

Turn the dough out onto a lightly floured surface and gently knead it into a ball. Flatten the dough into a disk, wrap it in plastic wrap, and refrigerate for at least 30 minutes.

Preheat your oven to 375°F (190°C). Roll out the chilled dough on a lightly floured surface into a circle large enough to fit into a 9-inch pie dish. Carefully transfer the dough to the pie dish, trimming any excess and crimping the edges as desired. Place the pie crust in the refrigerator while you prepare the filling.

In a large mixing bowl, whisk together the corn syrup, brown sugar, eggs, melted butter, vanilla extract, and salt until well combined.

Arrange the pecan halves evenly over the bottom of the prepared pie crust.

Pour the filling mixture over the pecans, ensuring they are evenly coated.

Place the pie in the preheated oven and bake for 40-50 minutes, or until the filling is set and the crust is golden brown. If the crust edges start to brown too quickly, you can cover them with aluminum foil.

Once baked, remove the pie from the oven and let it cool completely before serving. Enjoy your delicious pecan pie with crust!

plum pie

The history of plum pie traces back to ancient times when plums were a popular fruit across various regions of the world. Plums are believed to have originated in regions of Eastern Europe and Asia, with evidence of their cultivation dating back thousands of years.

Ingredients:

1 ½ pounds of ripe plums, pitted and sliced

200g granulated sugar

2 tablespoons cornstarch

1 teaspoon ground cinnamon

1/4 teaspoon ground nutmeg

1/4 teaspoon salt

1 tablespoon lemon juice

1 single pie crust pastry (store-bought or homemade)

1 tablespoon unsalted butter, cut into small pieces

1 egg beaten with 1 tablespoon water (for egg wash)

Granulated sugar, for sprinkling

Instructions:

Preheat your oven to 375°F (190°C).

In a large mixing bowl, combine the sliced plums, granulated sugar, cornstarch, cinnamon, nutmeg, salt, and lemon juice. Toss everything together until the plums are evenly coated. Let the mixture sit for about 15 minutes to allow the flavors to meld.

Roll out the pie pastry on a lightly floured surface to fit into a 9-inch pie dish. Carefully transfer the rolled-out pastry to the pie dish, gently pressing it into the bottom and sides.

Pour the plum filling into the prepared pie crust, spreading it out evenly. Dot the top of the filling with small pieces of butter.

If desired, you can create a decorative edge by folding the excess pastry over the edges of the filling.

Brush the edges of the crust with the egg wash and sprinkle them with granulated sugar for a golden, crispy finish.

Place the pie on a baking sheet (to catch any drips) and bake in the preheated oven for 45 to 50 minutes, or until the crust is golden brown and the filling is bubbling.

Once baked, remove the pie from the oven and let it cool on a wire rack for at least 1 hour before slicing and serving.

Serve the plum pie warm or at room temperature, optionally with a scoop of vanilla ice cream or a dollop of whipped cream.

Enjoy your homemade pie!

key lime pie

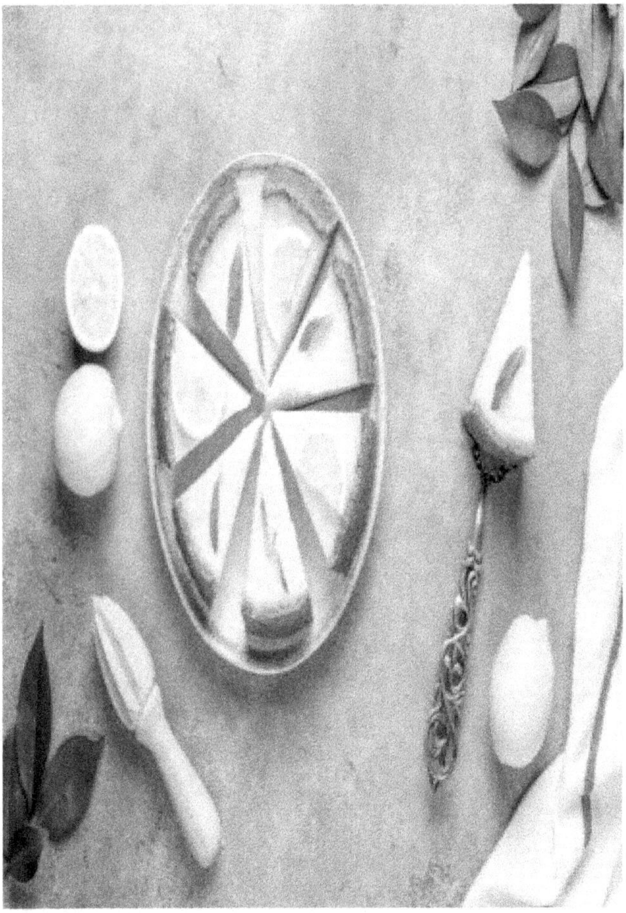

Key lime pie is a classic dessert originating from the Florida Keys, particularly associated with Key West. It typically consists of a graham cracker crust filled with a creamy, tangy filling made from key lime juice, sweetened condensed milk, and egg yolks. The pie is then topped with whipped cream or meringue and garnished with lime zest or slices.

Key limes, also known as Mexican or West Indian limes, are smaller and more acidic than the common Persian limes found in most grocery stores. They are the traditional choice for making authentic key lime pie, although Persian lime juice is often used as a substitute due to availability.

The pie is known for its refreshing flavor and creamy texture, with the tartness of the lime balanced by the sweetness of the condensed milk. It's a popular dessert in the southern United States and beyond, enjoyed by many for its unique taste and simple yet satisfying composition.

Ingredients:

For the crust:

1 1/2 cups graham cracker crumbs (about 10-12 whole graham crackers)

1/4 cup granulated sugar

6 tablespoons unsalted butter, melted

For the filling:

1 can (14 ounces) sweetened condensed milk

4 large egg yolks

1/2 cup fresh key lime juice (about 16-20 key limes), or bottled key lime juice if fresh is unavailable

For the topping (optional):

1 cup heavy whipping cream

2 tablespoons powdered sugar

Lime zest, for garnish

Instructions:

Preheat your oven to 350°F (175°C).

In a bowl, mix together the graham cracker crumbs, granulated sugar, and melted butter until well combined. Press the mixture firmly into the bottom and up the sides of a 9-inch pie dish to form the crust.

Bake the crust in the preheated oven for 10-12 minutes, or until lightly golden. Remove from the oven and let it cool while you prepare the filling. Leave the oven on.

In another bowl, whisk together the sweetened condensed milk and egg yolks until smooth. Gradually add in the key lime juice, whisking continuously until well combined.

Pour the filling into the cooled crust and spread it out evenly.

Bake the pie in the oven for 15-17 minutes, or until the edges are set but the center is still slightly jiggly.

Remove the pie from the oven and let it cool to room temperature. Once cooled, refrigerate for at least 2 hours, or until fully chilled and set.

If desired, whip the heavy cream and powdered sugar together until stiff peaks form. Spread or pipe the whipped cream onto the chilled pie.

Garnish with lime zest before serving.

Slice and enjoy your delicious homemade Key Lime Pie!

Remember, fresh key lime juice is ideal for the best flavor, but if you can't find key limes, bottled key lime juice works as a substitute. Enjoy your pie!

custard pie

A custard pie is a dessert consisting of a pastry crust filled with a sweet and creamy custard mixture. The custard is typically made with eggs, milk or cream, sugar, and flavorings such as vanilla or nutmeg. The pie is baked until the custard sets and the crust is golden brown. Custard pies can be served warm or cold, often with a dollop of whipped cream or a sprinkle of powdered sugar on top. They are a classic dessert enjoyed in many cultures around the world.

Ingredients

1 1/4 cups all-purpose flour

1/2 teaspoon salt

1/2 cup (1 stick) cold unsalted butter, cut into small cubes

3-4 tablespoons ice water

Ingredients for the custard filling:

4 large eggs

1/2 cup granulated sugar

2 cups whole milk

1 teaspoon vanilla extract

1/4 teaspoon salt

Ground nutmeg or cinnamon for sprinkling (optional)

Instructions for the pie crust:

In a large mixing bowl, combine the all-purpose flour and salt.

Add the cold cubed butter to the flour mixture. Using a pastry cutter or your fingers, work the butter into the flour until the mixture resembles coarse crumbs with some pea-sized pieces of butter remaining.

Gradually add the ice water, one tablespoon at a time, mixing with a fork until the dough begins to come together. Be careful not to add too much water; the dough should be just moist enough to hold together when pinched.

Shape the dough into a ball, flatten it into a disk, and wrap it tightly in plastic wrap. Refrigerate the dough for at least 30 minutes before rolling it out.

Instructions for assembling and baking the pie:

Preheat your oven to 375°F (190°C).

On a lightly floured surface, roll out the chilled pie crust into a circle about 12 inches in diameter. Carefully transfer the rolled-out crust to a 9-inch pie dish. Trim any excess dough hanging over the edges and crimp the edges as desired.

In a medium-sized mixing bowl, whisk together the eggs, sugar, vanilla extract, and salt until well combined.

Heat the milk in a saucepan over medium heat until it is just starting to simmer. Remove from heat.

Slowly pour the hot milk into the egg mixture, whisking constantly to temper the eggs and prevent them from scrambling.

Once the milk and egg mixture are fully combined, pour it into the prepared pie crust.

Optionally, sprinkle ground nutmeg or cinnamon on top of the custard for added flavor.

Carefully transfer the pie to the preheated oven and bake for 40-45 minutes, or until the custard is set and the crust is golden brown.

Remove the pie from the oven and allow it to cool completely before serving. You can serve it warm or chilled, with whipped cream or fresh fruit if desired.

Enjoy your delicious homemade
custard pie with crust!

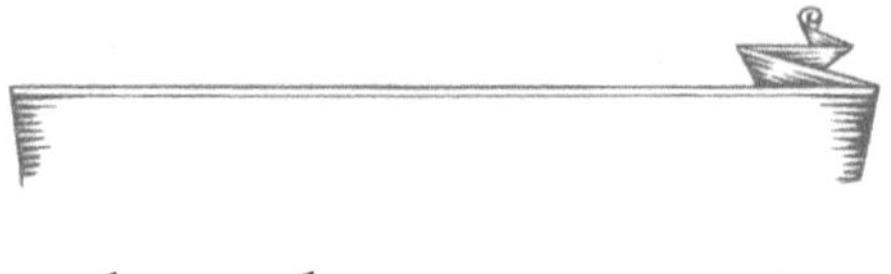

chocolate cream pie

Chocolate cream pie is a delicious dessert consisting of a flaky pie crust filled with a rich, creamy chocolate pudding-like filling, topped with whipped cream or meringue. It's a classic American dessert that's loved for its indulgent chocolate flavor and smooth texture.

Ingredients:

For the Pie Crust:

1 1/4 cups all-purpose flour

1/2 teaspoon salt

1/2 cup (1 stick) cold unsalted butter, cut into small pieces

2-4 tablespoons ice water

For the Chocolate Filling:

1 cup granulated sugar

1/4 cup cornstarch

1/4 teaspoon salt

4 large egg yolks

2 1/2 cups whole milk

4 ounces bittersweet chocolate, chopped

2 tablespoons unsalted butter

1 teaspoon vanilla extract

For the Topping:

Whipped cream or meringue

Instructions:

1. Make the Pie Crust:

In a food processor, combine the flour and salt. Add the cold butter pieces and pulse until the mixture resembles coarse crumbs.

Gradually add ice water, 1 tablespoon at a time, and pulse until the dough comes together and forms a ball.

Flatten the dough into a disk, wrap it in plastic wrap, and refrigerate for at least 30 minutes.

Preheat the oven to 375°F (190°C). Roll out the chilled dough on a floured surface and fit it into a 9-inch pie dish. Trim and crimp the edges, then prick the bottom of the crust with a fork.

Line the crust with parchment paper and fill with pie weights or dried beans. Bake for about 15 minutes. Remove the weights and parchment paper, then continue baking for another 10-15 minutes, or until the crust is golden brown. Let it cool completely.

2. Make the Chocolate Filling:

In a medium saucepan, whisk together the sugar, cornstarch, salt, and egg yolks until well combined.

Gradually whisk in the milk until smooth.

Place the saucepan over medium heat and cook, stirring constantly, until the mixture thickens and comes to a boil.

Remove the saucepan from the heat and stir in the chopped chocolate, butter, and vanilla extract until the chocolate and butter are melted and the mixture is smooth.

Pour the chocolate filling into the cooled pie crust. Smooth the top with a spatula and place plastic wrap directly on the surface to prevent a skin from forming. Refrigerate for at least 4 hours or until set.

3. Add the Topping:

Before serving, top the chilled pie with whipped cream or meringue.

Slice and serve chilled. Enjoy your delicious homemade chocolate cream pie!

Feel free to adjust the sweetness or richness of the filling according to your preference. You can also customize the topping by adding chocolate shavings or cocoa powder for an extra chocolatey touch.

coconut cream pie

Coconut cream pie is a delicious dessert consisting of a flaky pie crust filled with a rich, creamy coconut custard filling, topped with whipped cream and toasted coconut flakes.

Ingredients:

For the crust:

1 1/4 cups all-purpose flour

1/2 teaspoon salt

1/2 cup cold unsalted butter, cubed

2-4 tablespoons ice water

For the filling:

1 cup sweetened shredded coconut

2 cups coconut milk

1 cup whole milk

3/4 cup granulated sugar

1/4 cup cornstarch

1/4 teaspoon salt

4 large egg yolks

2 tablespoons unsalted butter

1 teaspoon vanilla extract

For the topping:

1 cup heavy cream

2 tablespoons powdered sugar

1/2 teaspoon vanilla extract

Toasted coconut flakes for garnish

Instructions:

Preheat your oven to 375°F (190°C).

To make the crust, in a food processor, combine the flour and salt. Add the cold cubed butter and pulse until the mixture resembles coarse crumbs. Slowly add ice water, one tablespoon at a time, and pulse until the dough comes together.

Transfer the dough to a floured surface and roll it out into a circle slightly larger than your pie dish. Carefully transfer the dough to the pie dish, trim any excess, and crimp the edges. Prick the bottom and sides of the crust with a fork. Place parchment paper over the crust and fill with pie weights or dried beans. Bake for about 15 minutes or until the crust is lightly golden. Remove the weights and parchment paper and bake for an additional 10 minutes until the crust is fully cooked. Let it cool completely.

To make the filling, spread the shredded coconut on a baking sheet and toast it in the oven for about 5-7 minutes, stirring occasionally, until lightly golden. Set aside.

In a saucepan, combine the coconut milk, whole milk, and half of the sugar. Bring to a simmer over medium heat.

In a separate bowl, whisk together the remaining sugar, cornstarch, salt, and egg yolks until smooth.

Gradually pour the hot milk mixture into the egg mixture, whisking constantly. Return the mixture to the saucepan and cook over medium heat, whisking constantly, until thickened, about 2-3 minutes. Remove from heat and stir in the butter, vanilla extract, and toasted coconut.

Pour the filling into the cooled pie crust and smooth the top. Cover with plastic wrap, pressing it directly onto the surface of the filling to prevent a skin from forming. Chill in the refrigerator for at least 4 hours, or until set.

Before serving, make the whipped cream topping. In a chilled bowl, whip the heavy cream, powdered sugar, and vanilla extract until stiff peaks form.

Spread the whipped cream over the chilled pie and sprinkle with toasted coconut flakes. Serve and enjoy your delicious coconut cream pie!

This recipe yields a classic coconut cream pie that's sure to impress your friends and family. Feel free to adjust the sweetness or coconut flavor to your preference.

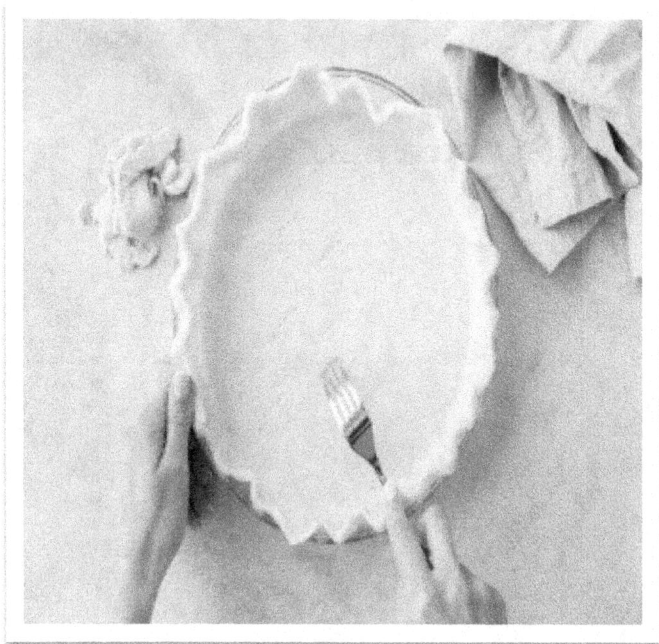

mixed berry pie

Mixed berry pie is a delicious dessert made with a combination of different types of berries, such as strawberries, blueberries, raspberries, and blackberries.

Ingredients:

For the pie crust:

2 1/2 cups all-purpose flour

1 cup (2 sticks) unsalted butter, cold and cubed

1 teaspoon salt

1 tablespoon granulated sugar

6-8 tablespoons ice water

For the filling:

4 cups mixed berries (strawberries, blueberries, raspberries, blackberries)

1/2 cup granulated sugar (adjust according to sweetness of berries)

1/4 cup cornstarch

1 tablespoon lemon juice

1 teaspoon vanilla extract

1/4 teaspoon ground cinnamon (optional)

1 egg, beaten (for egg wash)

Coarse sugar for sprinkling (optional)

Instructions:

Prepare the pie crust: In a large mixing bowl, combine the flour, salt, and sugar. Add the cold cubed butter. Using a pastry cutter or your hands, work the butter into the flour mixture until it resembles coarse crumbs with pea-sized pieces of butter.

Gradually add ice water, 1 tablespoon at a time, mixing gently with a fork, until the dough starts to come together. Be careful not to overwork the dough.

Divide the dough into two equal portions, shape each portion into a disk, wrap them in plastic wrap, and refrigerate for at least 1 hour, or until firm.

Preheat the oven to 375°F (190°C).

In a large mixing bowl, combine the mixed berries, sugar, cornstarch, lemon juice, vanilla extract, and ground cinnamon (if using). Toss gently until the berries are evenly coated.

Roll out one disk of dough on a lightly floured surface into a circle about 12 inches in diameter. Carefully transfer the rolled-out dough to a 9-inch pie dish, gently pressing it into the bottom and sides.

Pour the berry filling into the prepared pie crust.

Roll out the second disk of dough and place it over the filled pie. Trim any excess dough hanging over the edges and crimp the edges to seal. Cut a few slits on the top crust to allow steam to escape.

Brush the top crust with the beaten egg and sprinkle with coarse sugar, if desired.

Place the pie on a baking sheet (to catch any drips) and bake in the preheated oven for 45-50 minutes, or until the crust is golden brown and the filling is bubbling.

Allow the pie to cool completely before slicing and serving. Enjoy your delicious mixed berry pie!

Feel free to adjust the type and amount of berries and sugar according to your preference. You can also add a scoop of vanilla ice cream or whipped cream on top when serving for an extra indulgent treat.

Lemon icebox pie

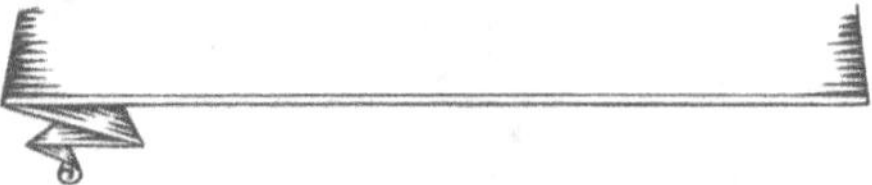

Icebox pie is a type of pie that is not baked, but instead, it sets in the refrigerator or freezer. It typically consists of a crumb or pastry crust filled with a creamy, often chilled filling. The filling can vary widely and may include ingredients like whipped cream, pudding, gelatin, custard, or even fruit. Popular variations include key lime pie, lemon icebox pie, and chocolate icebox pie. These pies are popular for their simplicity and refreshing taste, especially during warmer months. They are often served chilled and can be garnished with whipped cream, fruit, or chocolate shavings.

Ingredients:

For the crust:

1 1/2 cups graham cracker crumbs

1/4 cup granulated sugar

6 tablespoons unsalted butter, melted

For the filling:

1 (14-ounce) can sweetened condensed milk

4 large egg yolks

1/2 cup key lime juice (freshly squeezed is best, but bottled can work too)

1 tablespoon key lime zest

For the topping (optional):

Whipped cream

Additional lime zest or lime slices for garnish

Instructions:

Prepare the crust:

Preheat your oven to 350°F (175°C).

In a mixing bowl, combine the graham cracker crumbs, sugar, and melted butter until the mixture resembles wet sand.

Press the mixture firmly into the bottom and up the sides of a 9-inch pie dish.

Bake the crust for about 10 minutes, until lightly golden. Remove from the oven and let it cool completely.

Make the filling:

In a separate mixing bowl, whisk together the sweetened condensed milk, egg yolks, key lime juice, and key lime zest until well combined.

Pour the filling mixture into the cooled pie crust.

Chill the pie:

Place the pie in the refrigerator to chill for at least 4 hours, or until set. For a firmer texture, you can also place it in the freezer for a couple of hours.

Serve:

Once the pie is set, you can optionally top it with whipped cream and additional lime zest or lime slices for garnish.

Slice and serve chilled. Enjoy!

Note: If you can't find key limes, regular lime juice and zest can be used as a substitute. Additionally, you can adjust the sweetness or tartness of the pie by varying the amount of lime juice used.

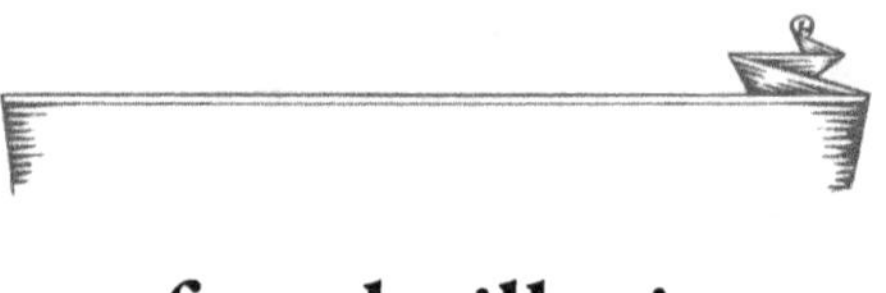

french silk pie

French silk pie is a delicious dessert consisting of a rich and creamy chocolate filling in a flaky pie crust, typically topped with whipped cream or chocolate shavings. The filling is made by whipping together butter, sugar, melted chocolate, eggs, and sometimes a splash of vanilla extract until it becomes smooth and silky in texture. This luxurious dessert is often served chilled, allowing the filling to set properly before slicing and serving. It's a popular choice for special occasions or simply as a treat for chocolate lovers.

Ingredients:

For the pie crust:

1 1/4 cups all-purpose flour

1/2 teaspoon salt

1/2 cup cold unsalted butter, cut into small cubes

1/4 cup ice water

For the filling:

1 cup unsalted butter, softened

1 1/2 cups granulated sugar

4 ounces unsweetened chocolate, melted and cooled

2 teaspoons vanilla extract

4 large eggs

For garnish (optional):

Whipped cream

Chocolate shavings or cocoa powder

Instructions:

Prepare the crust:

In a food processor, combine the flour and salt. Add the cold butter cubes and pulse until the mixture resembles coarse crumbs.

Gradually add the ice water, 1 tablespoon at a time, pulsing until the dough just begins to come together.

Turn the dough out onto a lightly floured surface and shape it into a disk. Wrap in plastic wrap and refrigerate for at least 1 hour.

Preheat your oven to 375°F (190°C).

Roll out the dough on a floured surface to fit a 9-inch pie dish. Press the dough into the dish and trim any excess. Prick the bottom of the crust with a fork.

Line the crust with parchment paper and fill it with pie weights or dried beans.

Bake for 15 minutes. Remove the weights and parchment paper, then bake for an additional 10-15 minutes, or until the crust is golden brown. Allow to cool completely.

Make the filling:

In a large bowl, beat the softened butter and sugar until light and fluffy.

Gradually add the melted chocolate and vanilla extract, mixing until well combined.

Add the eggs, one at a time, beating well after each addition. Continue to beat the mixture for about 5 minutes, until it becomes thick and creamy.

Pour the filling into the cooled pie crust and smooth the top with a spatula.

Chill and garnish:

Refrigerate the pie for at least 4 hours, or until set.

Before serving, garnish with whipped cream and chocolate shavings or a dusting of cocoa powder, if desired.

Enjoy your delicious French silk pie!

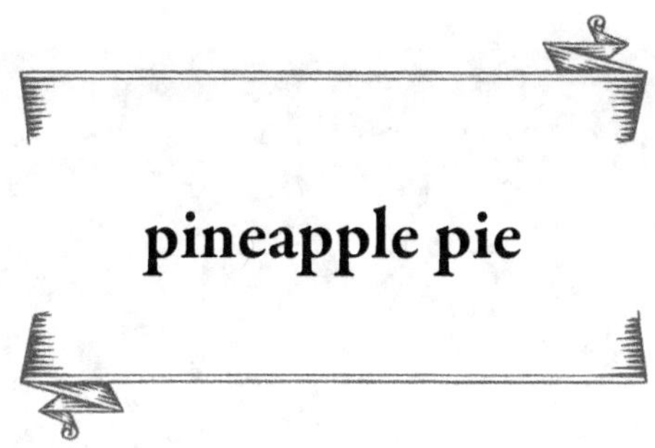

pineapple pie

P ineapple pie is a delicious dessert made with a flaky pie crust filled with a sweet and tangy pineapple filling.

Ingredients:

1 package of ready-made pie crusts (or you can make your own from scratch)

1 can (20 oz) crushed pineapple, drained

1 cup granulated sugar

1/4 cup all-purpose flour

1/4 teaspoon salt

1/2 teaspoon vanilla extract

2 tablespoons butter, diced into small pieces

1 egg (for egg wash)

Optional: whipped cream or vanilla ice cream for serving

Instructions:

Preheat your oven to 375°F (190°C).

Roll out one of the pie crusts and line a 9-inch pie dish with it. Trim any excess dough hanging over the edges.

In a large mixing bowl, combine the drained crushed pineapple, sugar, flour, salt, and vanilla extract. Mix until well combined.

Pour the pineapple mixture into the prepared pie crust and spread it out evenly. Dot the top with diced butter.

Roll out the second pie crust and place it over the filling. You can either place it over the filling as a whole crust or cut it into strips and create a lattice pattern.

Trim any excess dough and crimp the edges of the pie crusts together to seal.

Beat the egg in a small bowl and brush it over the top crust for a golden finish.

Use a sharp knife to make a few small slits in the top crust to allow steam to escape.

Place the pie on a baking sheet (to catch any drips) and bake in the preheated oven for 45-50 minutes, or until the crust is golden brown and the filling is bubbly.

Once baked, remove the pie from the oven and let it cool for at least 30 minutes before serving.

Serve slices of pineapple pie with whipped cream or vanilla ice cream if desired.

Enjoy your delicious homemade pineapple pie!

strawberry rhubarb pie

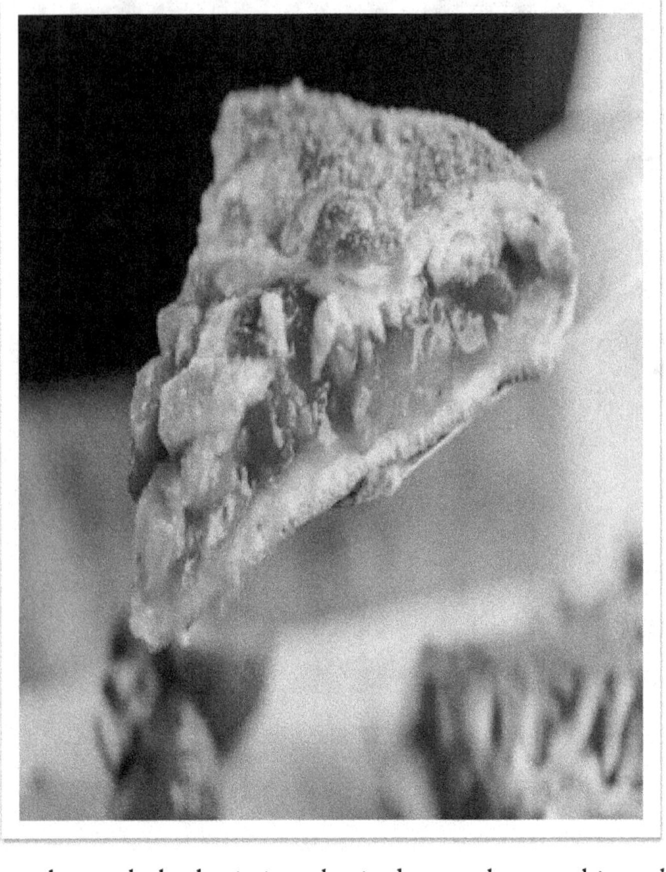

Strawberry rhubarb pie is a classic dessert that combines the sweet taste of strawberries with the tartness of rhubarb

Ingredients:

1 1/2 cups chopped rhubarb

1 1/2 cups sliced strawberries

1 cup granulated sugar

1/4 cup cornstarch

1 tablespoon lemon juice

1/2 teaspoon cinnamon

1/4 teaspoon nutmeg

1/4 teaspoon salt

2 pie crusts (store-bought or homemade)

Instructions:

Preheat your oven to 375°F (190°C).

In a large bowl, combine the chopped rhubarb, sliced strawberries, granulated sugar, cornstarch, lemon juice, cinnamon, nutmeg, and salt. Stir well to coat the fruit evenly.

Roll out one pie crust and line a 9-inch pie dish with it. Trim any excess crust hanging over the edges.

Pour the strawberry rhubarb filling into the prepared pie crust, spreading it out evenly.

Roll out the second pie crust and place it over the filling. You can either place the crust on top whole, make a lattice pattern, or cut shapes out of the crust for a decorative touch. Seal the edges by crimping them with a fork or your fingers.

Optional: Brush the top crust with milk or beaten egg for a golden finish.

Place the pie on a baking sheet (to catch any drips) and bake in the preheated oven for about 45-50 minutes, or until the crust is golden brown and the filling is bubbly.

Once baked, remove the pie from the oven and let it cool on a wire rack for at least 1 hour before serving. This allows the filling to set.

Serve the strawberry rhubarb pie warm or at room temperature, optionally with a scoop of vanilla ice cream or a dollop of whipped cream.

Enjoy your delicious homemade strawberry rhubarb pie!

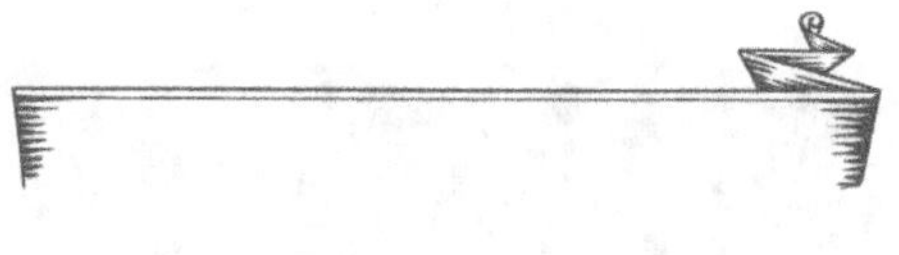

Lemon Meringue Tart

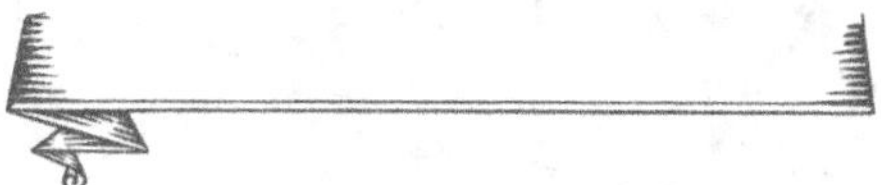

L emon meringue tart is a delightful dessert consisting of a buttery pastry crust filled with tangy lemon curd and topped with fluffy meringue.

Ingredients:

For the pastry crust:

1 1/4 cups all-purpose flour

1/4 cup granulated sugar

1/2 cup cold unsalted butter, cut into small cubes

1 egg yolk

1-2 tablespoons cold water

For the lemon filling:

3/4 cup freshly squeezed lemon juice

Zest of 2 lemons

1 cup granulated sugar

4 large eggs

1/2 cup unsalted butter, cut into small cubes

For the meringue:

4 large egg whites

1/2 cup granulated sugar

1/2 teaspoon cream of tartar

Instructions:

Prepare the pastry crust:

In a food processor, combine flour and sugar. Add cold cubed butter and pulse until the mixture resembles coarse crumbs.

Add the egg yolk and 1 tablespoon of cold water. Pulse again until the dough comes together. If needed, add another tablespoon of water.

Shape the dough into a disk, wrap it in plastic wrap, and refrigerate for at least 30 minutes.

Preheat your oven to 375°F (190°C). Roll out the chilled dough on a floured surface and line a tart pan with it. Prick the bottom of the crust with a fork. Line the crust with parchment paper and fill with pie weights or dried beans.

Bake for 15 minutes, then remove the parchment paper and weights, and bake for an additional 10-15 minutes, or until golden brown. Let it cool completely.

Make the lemon filling:

In a heatproof bowl, whisk together lemon juice, lemon zest, sugar, and eggs.

Place the bowl over a pot of simmering water (double boiler) and whisk constantly until the mixture thickens, about 8-10 minutes.

Remove from heat and whisk in the butter until smooth. Let the lemon curd cool slightly.

Pour the lemon curd into the cooled pastry crust and spread it evenly. Refrigerate while preparing the meringue.

Prepare the meringue:

In a clean, dry bowl, beat the egg whites with an electric mixer until foamy.

Add cream of tartar and continue to beat until soft peaks form.

Gradually add the sugar, a tablespoon at a time, while beating, until stiff, glossy peaks form.

Assemble and bake:

Preheat the oven to 350°F (175°C).

Spread the meringue over the lemon filling, making sure to seal the edges.

You can create peaks on the meringue using the back of a spoon or a spatula.

Bake the tart for about 15-20 minutes or until the meringue is lightly golden.

Let the tart cool completely before slicing and serving.

Enjoy your homemade lemon meringue tart!

chocolate peanut butter pie

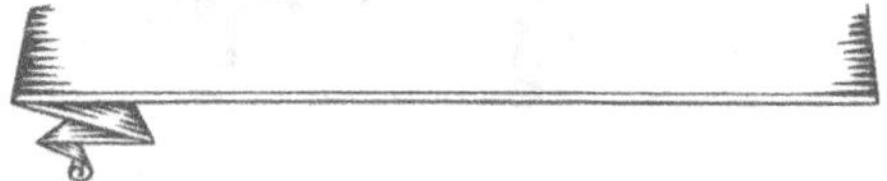

Chocolate peanut butter pie is a decadent dessert that combines two beloved flavors: chocolate and peanut butter.

Ingredients:

For the crust:

1 1/2 cups of chocolate cookie crumbs (you can use chocolate graham crackers or chocolate sandwich cookies)or graham crackers

6 tablespoons of melted butter

For the filling:

1 cup of creamy peanut butter

8 ounces of cream cheese, softened

1 cup of powdered sugar

1 teaspoon of vanilla extract

1 1/2 cups of heavy cream

For the topping (optional):

Chocolate shavings or chopped peanuts

Instructions:

1. Prepare the crust:

Preheat your oven to 350°F (175°C).

In a mixing bowl, combine the chocolate cookie crumbs and melted butter until well combined.

Press the mixture evenly into the bottom and up the sides of a 9-inch pie dish.

Bake the crust for 10 minutes, then remove it from the oven and let it cool completely.

2. Make the filling:

In a large mixing bowl, beat together the peanut butter, cream cheese, powdered sugar, and vanilla extract until smooth and creamy.

In a separate mixing bowl, whip the heavy cream until stiff peaks form.

Gently fold the whipped cream into the peanut butter mixture until well combined.

3. Assemble the pie:

Pour the peanut butter filling into the cooled crust, spreading it out evenly.

Smooth the top with a spatula.

If desired, sprinkle chocolate shavings or chopped peanuts over the top for decoration.

4. Chill and serve:

Cover the pie with plastic wrap and refrigerate for at least 4 hours, or until set.

Once chilled, slice and serve the pie cold.

Enjoy your delicious chocolate peanut butter pie! Feel free to customize it with additional toppings like whipped cream or chocolate drizzle, or even add chopped peanut butter cups into the filling for an extra indulgent twist.

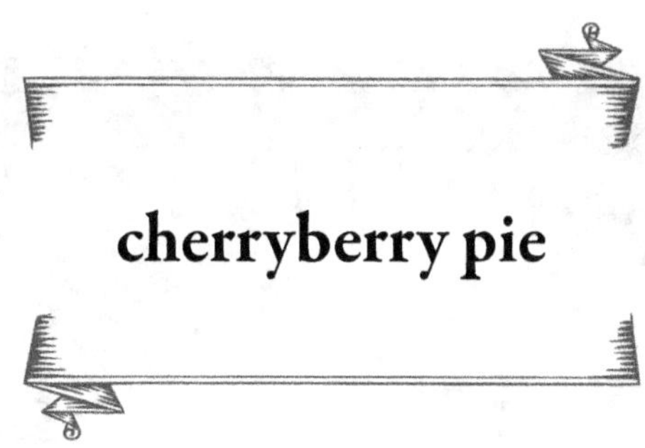

cherryberry pie

C herryberry pie is a delightful dessert that combines the flavors of cherries and other berries in a flaky crust.

Ingredients:

2 cups pitted cherries

2 cups mixed berries (such as blueberries, raspberries, blackberries)

3/4 cup granulated sugar

1/4 cup cornstarch

1 tablespoon lemon juice

1 teaspoon vanilla extract

1/4 teaspoon almond extract (optional)

1/4 teaspoon ground cinnamon

1/8 teaspoon salt

1 package (2 crusts) of ready-made pie crust or homemade pie crust

1 egg (for egg wash)

1 tablespoon water (for egg wash)

Additional sugar for sprinkling

Instructions:

Preheat your oven to 375°F (190°C).

In a large bowl, combine the cherries, mixed berries, sugar, cornstarch, lemon juice, vanilla extract, almond extract (if using), cinnamon, and salt. Gently toss until the fruit is evenly coated.

Roll out one pie crust and line a 9-inch pie dish with it. Trim any excess dough from the edges.

Pour the cherryberry filling into the prepared pie crust, spreading it out evenly.

Roll out the second pie crust and place it over the filling. You can make a lattice crust, a full crust with slits for venting, or any other decorative design you prefer. Seal the edges by crimping them with a fork or your fingers.

In a small bowl, beat the egg with water to make an egg wash. Brush the top crust with the egg wash.

Sprinkle some additional sugar over the top crust for extra sweetness and crunch.

Place the pie on a baking sheet (to catch any drips) and bake in the preheated oven for 45 to 55 minutes, or until the crust is golden brown and the filling is bubbling.

Once baked, remove the pie from the oven and allow it to cool on a wire rack for at least 1 hour before serving. This helps the filling to set.

Serve the cherryberry pie warm or at room temperature, optionally with a scoop of vanilla ice cream or a dollop of whipped cream.

Enjoy your delicious homemade cherryberry pie!

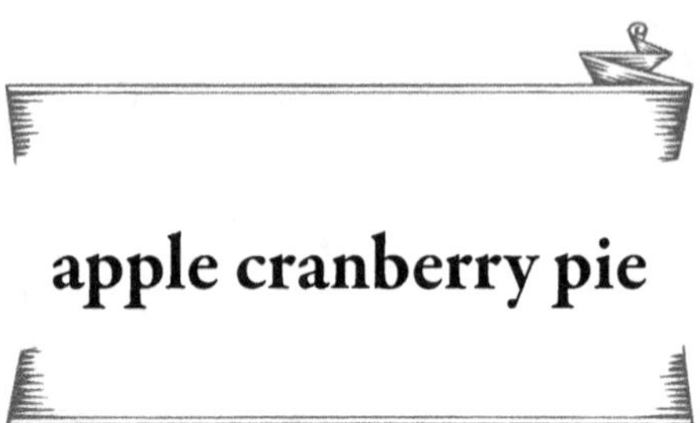

apple cranberry pie

Apple cranberry pie is a delightful dessert that combines the tartness of cranberries with the sweetness of apples, all baked in a flaky pie crust.

Ingredients:

2 pie crusts (store-bought or homemade)

4 cups of peeled, cored, and sliced apples (such as Granny Smith or Honeycrisp)

2 cups of fresh or frozen cranberries

3/4 cup of granulated sugar

1/4 cup of brown sugar

1/4 cup of all-purpose flour

1 teaspoon of ground cinnamon

1/4 teaspoon of ground nutmeg

1 tablespoon of lemon juice

1 tablespoon of butter, cut into small pieces

1 egg (for egg wash)

1 tablespoon of water (for egg wash)

Additional granulated sugar (for sprinkling)

Instructions:

Preheat your oven to 375°F (190°C).

Roll out one pie crust and place it in a 9-inch pie dish. Trim any excess crust hanging over the edges.

In a large mixing bowl, combine the sliced apples, cranberries, granulated sugar, brown sugar, flour, cinnamon, nutmeg, and lemon juice. Toss until the fruit is evenly coated.

Pour the apple-cranberry mixture into the prepared pie crust, spreading it out evenly. Dot the top of the filling with the pieces of butter.

Roll out the second pie crust and place it over the filling. Trim any excess crust and crimp the edges to seal the pie.

In a small bowl, beat the egg with water to make an egg wash. Brush the top crust with the egg wash, then sprinkle with a little granulated sugar for added sweetness and crunch.

Cut slits in the top crust to allow steam to escape during baking.

Place the pie on a baking sheet (to catch any drips) and bake in the preheated oven for 50-60 minutes, or until the crust is golden brown and the filling is bubbling.

If the crust starts to brown too quickly, you can cover the edges with aluminum foil to prevent burning.

Once baked, remove the pie from the oven and let it cool on a wire rack for at least 1 hour before slicing and serving.

Enjoy your delicious apple cranberry pie on its own or topped with a scoop of vanilla ice cream or a dollop of whipped cream!

banana caramel pie

Banana caramel pie is a delicious dessert that combines the rich flavors of bananas and caramel in a flaky pie crust

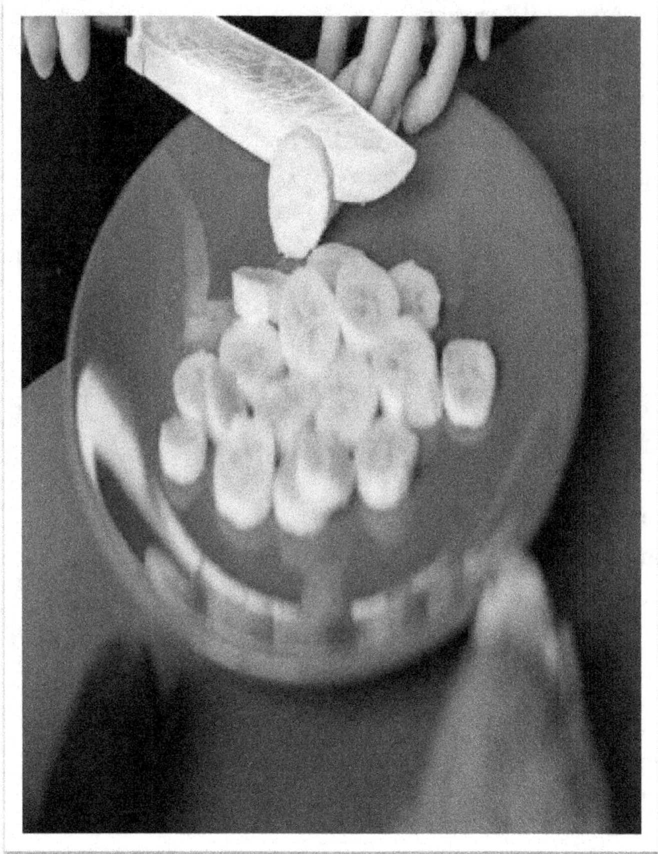

Ingredients:

For the pie crust:

1 1/4 cups all-purpose flour

1/2 teaspoon salt

1/2 cup unsalted butter, chilled and cubed

1/4 cup ice water

For the filling:

4 ripe bananas, sliced

1 cup caramel sauce (homemade or store-bought)

1 cup heavy cream

1/4 cup powdered sugar

1 teaspoon vanilla extract

Instructions:

For the pie crust:

In a large mixing bowl, combine the flour and salt.

Add the chilled cubed butter to the flour mixture.

Using a pastry cutter or your fingers, work the butter into the flour until the mixture resembles coarse crumbs.

Gradually add the ice water, one tablespoon at a time, mixing until the dough comes together.

Shape the dough into a disk, wrap it in plastic wrap, and refrigerate for at least 30 minutes.

For the filling:

Preheat your oven to 375°F (190°C).

Roll out the chilled pie crust on a floured surface and transfer it to a 9-inch pie dish. Crimp the edges as desired.

Blind bake the pie crust by lining it with parchment paper and filling it with pie weights or dried beans. Bake for 15-20 minutes, then remove the weights and parchment paper and bake for an additional 10 minutes, or until the crust is golden brown. Allow it to cool completely.

Spread half of the caramel sauce onto the bottom of the cooled pie crust.

Arrange the sliced bananas over the caramel sauce.

In a mixing bowl, whip the heavy cream, powdered sugar, and vanilla extract until stiff peaks form.

Gently fold the remaining caramel sauce into the whipped cream.

Spread the caramel whipped cream mixture over the sliced bananas in the pie crust.

Refrigerate the pie for at least 2 hours before serving to allow it to set.

Serve chilled and enjoy your delicious banana caramel pie!

caramel sauce

Ingredients:
1 cup granulated sugar
6 tablespoons unsalted butter, cut into pieces
1/2 cup heavy cream
1 teaspoon vanilla extract
Pinch of salt (optional)
Instructions:

Heat the sugar: In a heavy-bottomed saucepan, heat the granulated sugar over medium heat, stirring constantly with a wooden spoon or heatproof spatula. The sugar will start to form clumps and then melt into a thick, amber-colored liquid as it caramelizes. Be careful not to burn the sugar.

Add the butter: Once the sugar has melted completely and turned a deep amber color, add the butter, one piece at a time, stirring constantly until it's fully melted and incorporated into the caramel.

Add the cream: Carefully pour in the heavy cream while stirring constantly. Be cautious as the mixture may bubble up vigorously. Continue stirring until the caramel sauce is smooth and well combined.

Finish with vanilla and salt: Remove the saucepan from the heat and stir in the vanilla extract and a pinch of salt, if desired, to enhance the flavor.

Cool and store: Allow the caramel sauce to cool slightly before transferring it to a heatproof jar or container. Let it cool completely at room temperature before sealing and storing in the refrigerator. The caramel sauce will thicken as it cools.

Serve: Use the caramel sauce immediately as a topping for your banana caramel pie or any other dessert, or store it in the refrigerator for up to two weeks.

Feel free to garnish with additional caramel sauce or sliced bananas before serving, if desired. Enjoy!

CARAMEL

mincemeat pie

Mincemeat pie is a traditional British dessert pie filled with a mixture called mincemeat. Despite its name, modern mincemeat typically doesn't contain meat but is instead a combination of chopped dried fruits (such as raisins, currants, and sultanas), apples, candied citrus peel, spices (such as cinnamon, nutmeg, and cloves), sugar, suet (or vegetable shortening for vegetarian versions)Mincemeat pies are often served during the Christmas season in the UK, but they can be enjoyed year-round. The filling is encased in a pastry crust, usually shortcrust pastry or puff pastry, and baked until golden brown. Mincemeat pies can be served hot or cold, often with a dollop of cream, custard

Ingredients:

For the mincemeat filling:

1 cup raisins

1 cup currants

1 cup chopped dried apricots

1 cup chopped dried apples

1/2 cup chopped candied peel (such as orange or lemon)

1/2 cup chopped almonds or walnuts

1/2 cup brown sugar

1/2 cup unsalted butter, melted

Zest and juice of 1 lemon

Zest and juice of 1 orange

1 teaspoon ground cinnamon

1/2 teaspoon ground nutmeg

1/4 teaspoon ground cloves

1/4 teaspoon ground allspice

For the pastry:

2 1/2 cups all-purpose flour

1/2 teaspoon salt

1 cup unsalted butter, chilled and cubed

6-8 tablespoons ice water

Instructions:

In a large mixing bowl, combine all the ingredients for the mincemeat filling. Mix well until everything is evenly distributed. and stir to combine. Cover the bowl with plastic wrap and let it sit in the refrigerator overnight to allow the flavors to meld together.

To make the pastry, sift the flour and salt into a large mixing bowl. Add the chilled cubed butter. Using a pastry cutter or your fingertips, rub the butter into the flour until the mixture resembles coarse breadcrumbs.

Gradually add the ice water, a tablespoon at a time, mixing with a fork, until the dough comes together. Be careful not to overwork the dough. Shape the dough into a ball, wrap it in plastic wrap, and refrigerate for at least 30 minutes.

Preheat your oven to 375°F (190°C). Grease a 9-inch (23 cm) pie dish.

On a lightly floured surface, roll out two-thirds of the pastry dough into a circle large enough to line the bottom and sides of the pie dish. Carefully transfer the pastry to the pie dish and press it gently into place.

Spoon the mincemeat filling into the pastry-lined pie dish, spreading it out evenly.

Roll out the remaining pastry dough into a circle large enough to cover the pie. Place it over the filling, trim any excess pastry, and crimp the edges to seal. You can also use the excess pastry to decorate the top of the pie if desired.

Use a sharp knife to make a few small slits in the top crust to allow steam to escape during baking.

Bake the pie in the preheated oven for 35-40 minutes, or until the pastry is golden brown.

Allow the pie to cool slightly before serving. Serve warm or at room temperature, optionally with whipped cream, custard

Enjoy your homemade mincemeat pie!

gooseberry pie

Gooseberry pie is a delicious dessert made using gooseberries, a fruit that grows on a thorny bush and is known for its tart flavor.

Ingredients:

750g fresh gooseberries, washed and stems removed

200g granulated sugar (adjust according to the tartness of the berries)

3 tablespoons all-purpose flour

1 tablespoon lemon juice

1/4 teaspoon ground cinnamon (optional)

Pastry for double-crust pie (store-bought or homemade)

1 tablespoon butter, cut into small pieces

Milk or egg wash for brushing the crust (optional)

Granulated sugar for sprinkling (optional)

Instructions:

Preheat your oven to 400°F (200°C).

In a large bowl, combine the gooseberries, sugar, flour, lemon juice, and cinnamon (if using). Toss until the gooseberries are evenly coated.

Roll out half of the pastry and line a 9-inch pie dish with it. Trim the excess dough, leaving about a 1-inch overhang.

Pour the gooseberry filling into the prepared pie crust. Dot the filling with small pieces of butter.

Roll out the remaining pastry and place it over the filling. Trim any excess dough and crimp the edges to seal the pie. You can also use a fork to press down and seal the edges.

If desired, brush the top crust with milk or egg wash and sprinkle with granulated sugar for a shiny, crispy finish.

Cut slits or shapes into the top crust to allow steam to escape during baking.

Place the pie on a baking sheet (to catch any drips) and bake in the preheated oven for 40 to 45 minutes, or until the crust is golden brown and the filling is bubbly.

Once baked, remove the pie from the oven and allow it to cool on a wire rack for at least 30 minutes before slicing and serving.

Serve slices of gooseberry pie warm or at room temperature, optionally topped with whipped cream or vanilla ice cream.

Enjoy your homemade gooseberry pie!

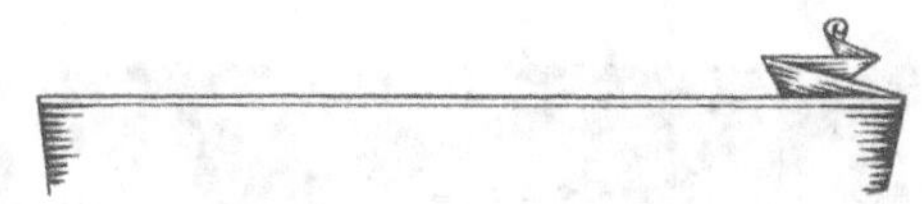

Chocolate Hazelnut Tarts

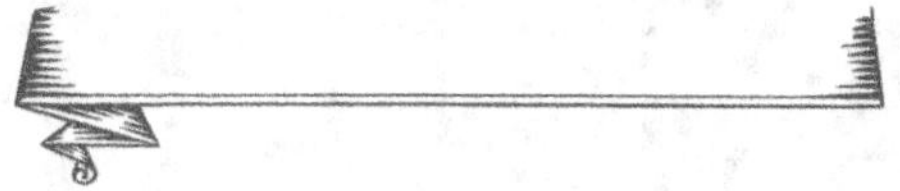

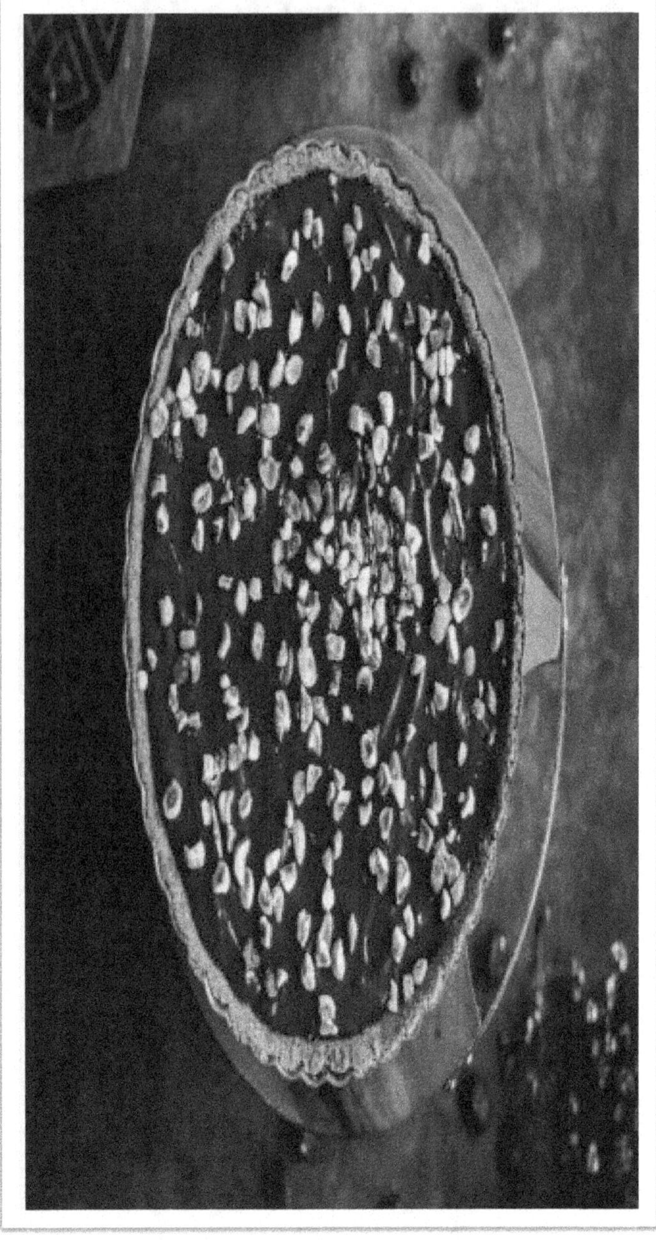

Chocolate hazelnut tarts are a delightful dessert featuring a rich, chocolatey filling complemented by the nutty flavor of hazelnuts.

Ingredients:

For the crust:

1 1/4 cups all-purpose flour

1/4 cup cocoa powder

1/4 cup granulated sugar

1/2 cup unsalted butter, cold and cut into small pieces

1 large egg yolk

2-3 tablespoons cold water

"You can replace the cocoa powder with an equal amount of all-purpose flour, ensuring the overall volume stays the same."

For the filling:

1 cup chocolate hazelnut spread (such as Nutella)

1/2 cup heavy cream

1/2 teaspoon vanilla extract

1/2 cup chopped hazelnuts, toasted

Instructions:

1. Prepare the crust:

In a food processor, combine the flour, cocoa powder, and sugar. Pulse to mix.

Add the cold butter pieces and pulse until the mixture resembles coarse crumbs.

Add the egg yolk and pulse again.

Gradually add cold water, one tablespoon at a time, pulsing until the dough comes together.

Turn the dough out onto a lightly floured surface and knead it gently until smooth. Shape it into a disc, wrap in plastic wrap, and refrigerate for at least 30 minutes.

2. Preheat the oven:

Preheat your oven to 350°F (175°C).

3. Prepare the tart shells:

Once the dough has chilled, roll it out on a lightly floured surface to about 1/8 inch thickness.

Use a round cutter or a glass to cut out circles slightly larger than your tart molds.

Press the dough circles into the tart molds, trimming any excess dough from the edges.

4. Blind bake the crust:

Line each tart shell with parchment paper and fill with pie weights or dried beans.

Bake in the preheated oven for 12-15 minutes, or until the crust is set.

Remove the parchment paper and weights and bake for an additional 5-7 minutes, or until the crust is dry and slightly crisp.

Remove from the oven and allow to cool completely.

5. Prepare the filling:

In a small saucepan, heat the heavy cream until it just begins to simmer.

Remove from heat and stir in the chocolate hazelnut spread and vanilla extract until smooth and well combined.

Let the mixture cool slightly.

6. Assemble the tarts:

Once the tart shells are completely cool, spoon the chocolate hazelnut filling into each shell, spreading it evenly.

Sprinkle chopped hazelnuts over the top of each tart.

7. Serve:

Allow the tarts to set in the refrigerator for at least 1 hour before serving.

Serve chilled, optionally garnished with a dusting of cocoa powder or a dollop of whipped cream.

Enjoy your delicious chocolate hazelnut tarts!

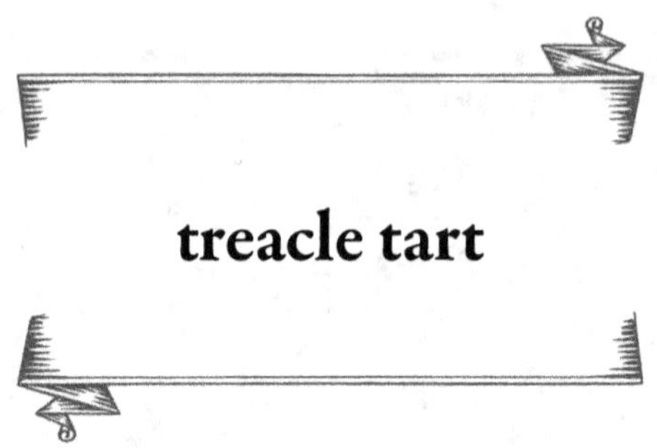

treacle tart

Treacle tart is a traditional British dessert consisting of a sweet pastry crust filled with a mixture of golden syrup (or treacle), breadcrumbs, lemon juice, and zest. It's usually served warm with a dollop of clotted cream, ice cream, or custard on the side. The filling is gooey and rich, with a sweet, caramel-like flavor from the golden syrup. Treacle tart is a beloved dessert, often enjoyed on its own or as part of a larger meal. It's particularly popular in England, especially for holiday celebrations like Christmas.

Ingredients:

For the pastry:

250g (2 cups) all-purpose flour

125g (1/2 cup) unsalted butter, cold and cubed

1 pinch of salt

1-2 tablespoons of cold water

For the filling:

450g (1 pound) golden syrup (or substitute with a mix of golden syrup and dark corn syrup if unavailable)

150g (1 1/2 cups) breadcrumbs (fresh or dried)

Zest and juice of 1 lemon

Optional: A splash of cream or milk (to bind the filling)

Instructions:

Preheat your oven to 180°C (350°F).

Start by making the pastry. In a large mixing bowl, sift the flour and salt together. Add the cold, cubed butter and rub it into the flour using your fingertips until the mixture resembles breadcrumbs.

Add 1-2 tablespoons of cold water gradually, mixing until the dough comes together. Be careful not to overwork the dough. Form it into a ball, wrap it in cling film, and chill it in the refrigerator for at least 30 minutes.

While the pastry is chilling, make the filling. In a saucepan, gently heat the golden syrup until it becomes runny. Remove from heat and stir in the breadcrumbs, lemon zest, and lemon juice. If the mixture seems too thick, you can add a splash of cream or milk to loosen it slightly.

Take the chilled pastry out of the refrigerator and roll it out on a lightly floured surface to fit your tart tin. Line the tin with the pastry, trimming off any excess. Prick the base with a fork.

Pour the filling into the pastry case, spreading it out evenly.

Bake in the preheated oven for 25-30 minutes, or until the pastry is golden brown and the filling is bubbling.

Allow the treacle tart to cool slightly before serving. Serve warm with clotted cream, ice cream, or custard.

Enjoy your delicious homemade treacle tart!

In closing, may this journey through the delectable world of pie-making leave you not only with a repertoire of tantalizing recipes but also with a deeper appreciation for the artistry, tradition, and joy that each slice brings. As you embark on your own culinary adventures, may your crusts be flaky, your fillings abundant, and your creations shared with love and laughter around tables filled with cherished company. Remember, in the realm of pie, there is always room for one more slice, one more story, and one more moment of pure delight. So, with rolling pin in hand and apron tied snug, let us continue to savor the simple pleasures and timeless traditions that make pie truly a masterpiece. Here's to the joy of baking and the sweetness of life. Bon appétit!

Don't miss out!

Visit the website below and you can sign up to receive emails whenever Dessert Dreamweaver publishes a new book. There's no charge and no obligation.

https://books2read.com/r/B-A-SJQCB-NMTZC

BOOKS2READ

Connecting independent readers to independent writers.

Also by Dessert Dreamweaver

Cookie Making Made Simple
Pies & Tarts A Delicious Slice of Life

www.ingramcontent.com/pod-product-compliance
Lightning Source LLC
Chambersburg PA
CBHW071323130726

47996CB00002B/596